HOME IS A HOLY PLACE

HOME IS A HOLY PLACE

Reflections, Prayers and Meditations
Inspired by the Ordinary

Mark G. Boyer

ACTA
ASSISTING CHRISTIANS TO ACT
PUBLICATIONS

Home Is a Holy Place: Reflections, Prayers and Meditations Inspired by the Ordinary
by Mark G. Boyer

Edited by Francine M. O'Connor
Cover by Tom Wright
Design and Typesetting by Garrison Publications

Scripture quotations are from the *New Revised Standard Version Bible: Catholic Edition*, copyright © 1993 and 1989 by the Division of Christian Education of the National Council of the Churches of Christ in the U.S.A. Used by permission. All rights reserved.

Published by: ACTA Publications
          Assisting Christians To Act
          4848 N. Clark Street
          Chicago, IL 60640
          773-271-1030

Library of Congress Catalog Number: 96-80171

ISBN: 0-87946-155-1

Printed in the United States of America

01 00 99   5 4 3 2

Contents

*Dedicated to
Sarah Osia,
my great-grandmother,
who taught me to find God
in the simple things of life.*

Introduction

Home is a holy place, a sanctuary where God is alive and active in the ordinary things and events that surround us. St. Paul wrote, "...Do you not know that your body is a temple of the Holy Spirit within you, which you have from God, and that you are not your own?" (1 Corinthians 6:19). Through the Holy Spirit dwelling within you, God enters your home and transforms that ordinary place into a shrine.

Home Is a Holy Place is designed to guide you into daily prayer experiences. Our secular society tends to separate the holy from the ordinary, proposing that prayer has no place in our daily lives, that it is best done in sacred surroundings and at extraordinary moments. This book challenges that proposal by offering, as the subtitle implies, reflections, prayers and meditations inspired by everyday items found in the home.

The book follows the alphabet from A to Z, with each reflection based on a household object or activity. A book arranged alphabetically is called an abecedarian, a word that also describes one who is learning the basics of an idea or theme—in this case, domestic spirituality or the holiness of the home.

This book is meant to be both prayerful and fun by illustrating how our home environment is charged with God's presence. Once we can recognize God's presence in the ordinary objects we see and use every day, we are led into a more intimate relationship. A walk through the rooms of our home will be a walk taken with God.

Each exercise in this book consists of five parts: Title, Scripture, Reflection, Meditation and Prayer. The *Title* is an ordinary item from the home, each beginning with a successive letter of the alphabet. The *Scripture* section, taken from either the Old (Hebrew) Testament or the New (Christian) Testament, establishes these everyday items in our faith.

The *Reflection* is meant to stimulate your thoughts, help you to make a God connection, and inspire your awareness of God's presence in your home. The *Meditation* consists of questions to encourage personal contemplation or journaling to chronicle your spiritual growth.

Finally, the *Prayer,* designed to summarize the ideas presented in the Scripture selection, the reflection, and your own personal meditation, brings the exercise to a close.

It is my hope that, through this book, you will be awakened to God's presence in every room of your home as you go about the task of discovering the holy in the ordinary—every day of your life.

Do you not know that you are God's temple and that God's Spirit dwells in you? If anyone destroys God's temple, God will destroy that person. For God's temple is holy, and you are that temple.

Corinthians 3:16-17

Apron

*So when the woman saw that the tree was good for food,
that it was a delight to the eyes, and that the tree was to
be desired to make one wise, she took of its fruit and ate;
and she also gave some to her husband, who was with
her, and he ate. Then the eyes of both were opened, and
they knew that they were naked; and they sewed fig
leaves together and made loincloths for themselves
(Genesis 3:6-7).*

Reflection

I have vivid memories of my great-grandmother, who
always wore a full apron over her long dress. Great-grandmother's apron was so much a part of her daily dress that
she would have felt naked without it. In its one large pocket
she carried her coin purse, handkerchief and rosary. Only on
Sunday did she remove the apron, and only then to attend
Mass in our local parish church.

Aprons are not common apparel today, but most of us
still use some sort of protective clothing while working.
When we are cooking or cleaning or officiating at the out-
door grill, we may tie a dish towel at our waists or put on a
full bib apron. While working in the yard, we might don jeans
and a sweatshirt. Chefs, waiters and waitresses, fire-
fighters, and construction workers can be identified by the
clothing that protects them on the job.

After their act of disobedience, Adam and Eve fash-
ioned a type of apron for themselves to cover their nakedness and hide their sin from their Creator. Then, writes the
author of the Book of Genesis, "...The Lord God made gar-

ments of skins for the man and for his wife, and clothed them" (Genesis 3:21). Thus, after first protecting them from the elements, God sent them into the world.

When we dress to cook, clean or work, we can recall how God clothes us in divine protection day after day. May our clothing be a reminder of God's watch over us.

Meditation

- When was the last time you wore some sort of protective clothing?
- Make a list of the ways in which it protected you.
- How does God protect you? Keep a running list throughout your day.

Prayer

God of creation, you formed man and woman in your own image and blew into them the breath of life. You entrusted to their care everything you had made. Even when they sinned, you continued to protect them by dressing them in garments of skins. When I dress to cook, to clean, or to work, awaken in me an awareness of your great love and an appreciation for the protection you give every day of my life. I ask this in the name of Jesus, your Son, who lives and reigns with you and the Holy Spirit, one God, for ever and ever. Amen.

Bathtub

Naaman, commander of the army of the king of Aram, was a great man and in high favor with his master, because by him the Lord had given victory to Aram. The man, though a mighty warrior, suffered from leprosy....Naaman came with his horses and chariots, and halted at the entrance of Elisha's house. Elisha sent a messenger to him, saying, "Go, wash in the Jordan seven times, and your flesh shall be restored, and you shall be clean."...So he went down and immersed himself seven times in the Jordan, according to the word of the man of God; his flesh was restored like the flesh of a young boy, and he was clean (2 Kings 5:1, 9-10, 14).

Reflection

Have you ever settled down into a relaxing bubble bath at the end of a long, hard day? Soothed by the warm water, the day's problems and troubles seem to disappear like floating bubbles. Whirlpools, jacuzzis, and hot tubs are all instruments of healing that massage tired muscles and ease aches and pains with the swirl of water and the gurgle of air jets. Steam baths and saunas use heat to relax and restore energy.

The healing of Naaman's leprosy in the waters of the Jordan was a direct result of his faith. Naaman, though not an Israelite, believed in the power of Elisha's God. By plunging into the river, he was healed. Emerging from the river, he stepped into a new life.

Our baths or showers can also be instruments of spiritual healing. As we soak in the calming waters or feel the warm shower soothing us, we relive the moment of our baptism, when we were immersed into or sprinkled with the waters of the font and raised to new life.

Each time you bathe or shower, renew again your baptismal promises and remember the healing love of Jesus Christ.

Meditation

- Recall the last long, healing bath you took.
- What did you think about?
- Of what were you healed?
- If you seldom spend time luxuriating in the tub, plan right now to indulge yourself in the name of inner healing.

Prayer

God of the waters, through the word of your prophet, Elisha, Naaman entered into the Jordan as a leper and, after seven plunges in the death-dealing river, emerged cleansed and healed. On the day of my baptism, you immersed me into a watery tomb and raised me up to new life with Christ, your Son. Make me grow in awareness of the daily dying and rising to which you call me through Jesus Christ, who lives and reigns with you and the Holy Spirit, one God, for ever and ever. Amen.

Bed

What do people gain from all the toil
at which they toil under the sun?
A generation goes, and a generation comes,
but the earth remains forever.
The sun rises and the sun goes down,
and hurries to the place where it rises.
...All things are wearisome;
more than one can express;
the eye is not satisfied with seeing
or the ear filled with hearing.
What has been is what will be,
and what has been done is what will be done;
there is nothing new under the sun.

Ecclesiastes 1:2-9

Reflection

In our beds, we find the ideal place to pray and reflect on our lives. Each night, as we slip under the covers, all that surrounds us slips away. Drifting into sleep, we enter into a peaceful but passing experience of death from which we are resurrected each morning. Sleep refreshes us and gives us the energy to rise and face another day. Even a simple afternoon nap can put us in contact with this rhythm in our lives.

Sleep teaches us to put aside the anxieties of the day. The unwashed load of laundry, the missed deadline, all those small and not-so-small irritations that seemed so important during the day are placed in perspective. We are with our God, who will watch over us as we sleep and give us a brand new day of resurrection when we wake.

Meditation

- When you go to bed this evening, close your eyes and consider the following questions:

  What has this day brought for which I am thankful? for which I am sorry?

  How does the natural rhythm of sleep and rising prepare me for my death and resurrection?

Prayer

Lord God, guardian of my life, you never sleep. From the rising of the sun to its setting, you watch over me and protect me. You teach me to not fear death, but to embrace it and practice it daily through the rhythm of sleep and rising. Strengthen my faith and trust in your promise of resurrection. Upon my bed may I always praise you through your Son, Jesus Christ, who lives and reigns with you and the Holy Spirit, one God, for ever and ever. Amen.

Chair

[Bazalel] made a mercy seat of pure gold; two cubits and a half was its length, and a cubit and a half its width. He made two cherubim of hammered gold; at the two ends of the mercy seat he made them, one cherub at the one end, and one cherub at the other end; of one piece with the mercy seat he made the cherubim at its two ends. The cherubim spread out their wings above, overshadowing the mercy seat with their wings. They faced one another; the faces of the cherubim were turned toward the mercy seat (Exodus 37:6-9).

Reflection

The mercy seat of God was constructed on top of the ark of the covenant, which contained the two tablets of the law, possibly a jar of manna, and Aaron's staff. From this chair above the ark, God presided over the chosen people, Israel, and received the nation's offerings of atonement.

In biblical times, a chair symbolized authority. A king's throne signified dominion over his subjects. Decisions concerning life and death were rendered daily from a judge's bench, much as they are today. The expression, the Chair of Peter, indicates the teaching authority of the pope, and in church pews around the world we gather to celebrate God's loving authority over our hearts.

We spend most of our waking hours sitting—at tables, on couches and benches, in our cars, at our desks, in waiting rooms. We arrange the chairs in our dens or living rooms so family and friends can visit and talk comfortably. We circle our chairs around the dining room table to share food and conversation.

Most of us have a favorite chair, a familiar place to rest, watch television, and share time with our family or friends. Other chairs in our homes have particular functions, and some chairs are associated with events that helped to shape our lives.

Meditation

- Go through your home and make a list of the chairs in each room and how they are used.
- Record any memory you have that is associated with a particular chair.

Prayer

God of mercy, you once took your seat among your chosen people, Israel–leading, guiding and accepting sacrifices. In the fullness of time you sent us your only begotten Son, Jesus, who now sits at your right hand and will come again to sit upon his throne and judge the world. When I sit to pray, make me humble. When I sit to work, make me diligent. When I sit to eat, make me aware of your blessings. When I sit to rest, make me secure in your love. I ask this through Jesus Christ, your Son, who lives and reigns with you and the Holy Spirit, one God, for ever and ever. Amen.

Clock

*For everything there is a season and a time for every
    matter under heaven:*
a time to be born, and a time to die;
a time to plant, and a time to pluck up what is planted;
a time to kill, and a time to heal;
a time to break down, and a time to build up;
a time to weep, and a time to laugh;
a time to mourn, and a time to dance;
*a time to throw away stones, and a time to gather stones
    together;*
*a time to embrace, and a time to refrain from
    embracing;*
a time to seek, and a time to lose;
a time to keep, and a time to throw away;
a time to tear, and a time to sew;
a time to keep silence, and a time to speak;
a time to love, and a time to hate;
a time for war, and a time for peace.

Ecclesiastes 3:1-8

Reflection

Our days are ruled by clocks. Our bedroom alarm clock
wakes us; we time our meals by the clock on the range or
oven; ornate clocks decorate our living room walls or our
mantles. A time clock or desk clock signals it's time to begin
or end our working day. In bus stations and airports, clocks
help us to get where we are going on time.

Every time the hands of a clock circle the face,
twenty-four hours of life elapse. Digital numbers flash on
our watches, counting the seconds and minutes of our day.

A calendar is a yearly clock, dividing our lives into days, weeks and months.

We talk about losing time, finding time, looking for time, wasting time, spending time, making time, being ahead of time or behind time, killing time, passing time, or taking time—but we cannot stop time from happening. In our world, time matters, and we count every moment, day, week, month or year.

Not so with God. Eternity is not time-limited. Eventually, we too will pass beyond the boundaries of time and enter eternity. But for now, God gives us time to do what we must do in the world. Let's share our time with God, for time spent with God is time well spent.

Meditation

- Make an hour-by-hour outline of your daily routine. Be sure to indicate how much time you spend sleeping, eating, working and praying in twenty-four hours.
- Have you spent as much time with loved ones as you should?
- Are there better ways to use your precious gift of time?

Prayer

Eternal God, with you there is no time, but you gifted me with years, months, days, hours and minutes to serve you. You are with me at all times, when I weep and when I laugh, when I seek and when I lose. The face of my clock is a sign of your infinite love. Enable me to make each sacred moment a hymn of praise. I ask this through Jesus Christ, your Son, who lives and reigns with you and the Holy Spirit, one God, for ever and ever. Amen.

Door

"Listen! I am standing at the door, knocking; if you hear my voice and open the door, I will come in to you and eat with you, and you with me. To the one who conquers I will give a place with me on my throne, just as I myself conquered and sat down with my Father on his throne" (Revelation 3:20-21).

Reflection

Doors—every house has at least one and usually two; every room in every house has one; every building has one.

Through our doors, we and our families enter into our "sacred" space. The door to our private room is the gateway to our sanctuary, offering us the luxury of privacy. We can enter our own space, shut the door, and be alone to pray, to think, or just to be. Or we can invite friends in to visit and share companionship.

We decorate our doors with wreaths or posters to offer a welcoming sign for visitors. "No Smoking" or "No Soliciting" signs set personal limits for those who enter there.

An "open door" implies that a person is willing to share time with us ("My door is always open," a friend may say), while a closed door indicates we will have to wait or come back later.

Our hearts are like doors to our inner selves. We can close ourselves in and lose the joy of living, or we can throw ourselves open to the new and exciting world God has given us.

In order for anyone—including Jesus—to enter, our hearts must be open. Jesus waits patiently for our invitation, offering gifts of love and care.

Meditation

- List the people who came through the door of your home yesterday, including yourself.
- For each person, identify one gift that he or she brought into your home and shared with you.
- Stand in your doorway and look around. What items in your home indicate a warm welcome awaits you? What things indicate an unwillingness to be with others?

Prayer

Lord God, your door is always open when I call upon your name. Keep watch at the door of my lips, that no harsh words may exit there. Keep me secure in your love that I might not lock out the needs of your people. Let my mind be always open to your word and the welcome mat be out for your Son, Jesus, who knocks at my door and who lives and reigns with you and the Holy Spirit, one God, for ever and ever. Amen.

Electricity

[Jesus said to Nicodemus:] "The wind blows where it chooses, and you hear the sound of it, but you do not know where it comes from or where it goes. So it is with everyone who is born of the Spirit" (John 3:8).

Reflection

Throughout our homes, plugs and switches are hooked up to lamps, computers and household appliances. We flip a switch and a light comes on; flip down the same switch and the room is immediately darkened.

Unseen, but laced throughout the floors, walls and ceilings of our homes, wires carry electrical current to various plugs and switches. Electricity enters our homes by way of intertwined wires on the pole outside. Stand in front of the meter and watch the wheel spin as it measures the invisible current. Stop for a minute under a pole and listen to the hum, as electricity walks over the wires.

We use electrical energy to heat and cool our homes. It activates our TVs, radios and computers. It is invisible, but powerful. Touch a bare wire and we get a shock. Contact with a power line can mean severe injury, even death.

In John's Gospel, Jesus uses the wind to describe the Spirit to Nicodemus. You hear the sound of wind in the trees and feel it on your face, but like the electricity in your home you cannot see it. Today, as you listen to the hum of current moving through the electrical pole outside your home, remember and embrace the presence of the invisible Spirit within you.

The Spirit warms our hearts, feeds our spiritual hunger, and guides our lives. The Spirit fills us with light and motivates us to do what is right. The Spirit is our source of divine power, a pure gift from God. Through the Spirit we connect with God and plug into our source of eternal life.

Meditation

- Make a list of all the ways you use electricity.
- For each item on your list, indicate how it can help you understand the work of the Holy Spirit in your life and in the world.

Prayer

God of the mighty wind, at the beginning of time your Spirit hovered over the waters and brought forth order from chaos. After you created people in your own image and likeness, you blew the breath of life of your Spirit into them. Fill me with the gift of your Spirit and envelop me in your presence. Deepen my awareness of how you direct me toward your kingdom, where you live and reign with your Son, Jesus Christ, and the Holy Spirit, one God, for ever and ever. Amen.

Floor

As the people were filled with expectation, and all were questioning in their hearts concerning John, whether he might be the Messiah, John answered all of them by saying, "I baptize you with water; but one who is more powerful than I is coming; I am not worthy to untie the thong of his sandals. He will baptize you with the Holy Spirit and fire. His winnowing fork is in his hand, to clear his threshing floor and to gather the wheat into his granary; but the chaff he will burn with unquenchable fire" (Luke 3:15-17).

Reflection

The floors in our homes are usually made of wood and covered with carpet or tile. Carpeted floors accommodate people who sit, lie or crawl on them. A bathroom floor is tiled to resist moisture, while a garage floor is usually poured cement.

In biblical times, the floor of a home was dirt, the natural earth around which the house was built. While palace floors were made of fired clay and the rich had floors of stone, the floor of the ordinary homeowner was dried, hard, beaten, flat earth where families slept, played, ate, and sat around a fire in warm fellowship.

The threshing floor mentioned in our Scripture passage was where the farmer separated the wheat from the chaff. He would harvest the wheat stalks, lay them on the dirt floor, and lead the oxen over them. The heavy hooves disengaged the grain from the stalk and removed the husk (chaff). Then the farmer would take his winnowing fan, a fork-like shovel, and toss the chaff and wheat into the air. The heavier kernels fell to the floor, while the lighter, unusable chaff blew away. The wheat was gathered and ground into flour, and the chaff was swept up and burned.

John the Baptizer compared the threshing of wheat to the separation of the good people from the bad at the end of the world. John explained that Jesus would separate the good from the bad, heralding to the people that the end of the world was near and judgment had come upon the earth.

Meditation

- Can you think of ways the floors in your home are used to separate the good from the bad?
- Choose three different floors and list how this might be true.

Prayer

God in heaven, the clouds form the floor of your home. You gave the earth to your people that we might walk upon it, till it, and enjoy it. Give me a deep appreciation for all of your creation. Help me to always walk in the ways of Jesus, your Son, who will one day come to the threshing floor to separate the good from the bad. He lives and reigns with you and the Holy Spirit, one God, for ever and ever. Amen.

Furnace

Nebuchadnezzar in furious rage commanded that Shadrach, Meshach, and Abednego be brought in; so they brought those men before the king. Nebuchadnezzar said to them: "Is it true, O Shadrach, Meshach, and Abednego, that you do not serve my gods and you do not worship the golden statue that I have set up? Now if you are ready when you hear the sound of the horn, pipe, lyre, trigon, harp, drum, and entire musical ensemble to fall down and worship the statue that I have made, well and good. But if you do not worship, you shall immediately be thrown into a furnace of blazing fire, and who is the god that will deliver you out of my hands?"

Shadrach, Meshach, and Abednego answered the king, "O Nebuchadnezzar, we have no need to present a defense to you in this matter. If our God whom we serve is able to deliver us from the furnace of blazing fire and out of your hand, O king, let him deliver us" (Daniel 3:13-17).

Reflection

Most furnaces today use natural gas, oil or electricity to send hot air through ducts connected to the rooms in our homes. Older furnaces may have a boiler, which sends hot water through pipes to radiators. Our furnaces may be located in the basement or in a utility room or elsewhere in our home. They provide heat in the winter and sometimes air conditioning in the summer.

Blast furnaces are used in industry for smelting ore. You have probably seen pictures of a smelter on television or in a magazine. A huge cauldron of liquid metal is moved out of the white-hot flames of the furnace and poured into a mold. Once hardened and cooled, the metal is rolled into sheets and cut for commercial use.

In biblical times, furnaces were used to refine precious metals, removing impurities from gold and silver by melting them. But furnaces were also used for capital punishment. The convicted person was thrown into the furnace and burned alive. There was no escaping the flames, and the body was completely consumed.

Shadrach, Meshach and Abednego, the young men in the Book of Daniel, were punished for refusing to worship the king's idols. But they were seen walking around the furnace, untouched by the flames. The fire of God's love was greater than the flames of death.

Fire draws us together. Recall the warm feeling of sitting around a campfire or the way the crackle of a fire in the fireplace warms us on a cold winter's evening. The warmth provided by our furnaces reminds us of the warm circles of love and protection provided by our families and our God.

Meditation

- Identify the "circles of fire" that draw people together in your home.
- What recent, important event took place in each?

Prayer

God of fire, the fire of your love draws me into your circle of care and purifies my mind and heart. Protect me from all harm and send me the fire of your Spirit, who lives and reigns with you and your Son, Jesus Christ, one God, for ever and ever. Amen.

Grill

The LORD said to Moses and Aaron in the land of Egypt:
"...Tell the whole congregation of Israel...to take a lamb
for each family, a lamb for each household. Your lamb
shall be without blemish, a year-old male; you may take
it from the sheep or the goats....The whole assembled
congregation of Israel shall slaughter it at twilight. They
shall take some of the blood and put it on the two door-
posts and the lintel of the houses in which they eat it.
They shall eat the lamb that same night; they shall eat it
roasted over the fire with unleavened bread and bitter
herbs. Do not eat any of it raw or boiled in water, but
roasted over the fire....It is the passover of the Lord....
The blood shall be a sign for you on the houses where
you live: when I see the blood, I will pass over you...."
(Exodus 12:1, 3, 5-9, 11, 13).

Reflection

Today, most backyards contain a barbecue grill, perma-
nent or portable, fueled by charcoal or natural gas. With
family and friends, we cook steaks, chicken, hamburgers or
hot dogs on weekends or hot summer days or for any special
time of gathering and celebration.

At a Texas-style barbecue, a side of beef is turned
over an open flame and basted with sauce. The old westerns
show cowboys or ranch hands gathered around a fire with
food on a spit. An entire roasted pig with an apple in its
mouth brings to mind a Hawaiian luau.

God's instructions to Moses and Aaron for the Passover specify that the lamb is to be roasted before it is eaten and the blood smeared on the doorposts and lintel of every Israelite home. With this sign, God delivered the people from slavery and set them on the road to freedom.

Jesus is the new Passover lamb. When he was put to death on a cross, his blood delivered us from sin and set our feet on the road to his kingdom. Before he died, Jesus instructed his disciples to break bread and drink wine in remembrance of his passover from death to life. Today we celebrate his passover whenever we receive his body and blood.

Each time we prepare a special feast, on the grill or in our kitchens, we can relive the love of Jesus, our Passover lamb, and celebrate his promise of freedom in his kingdom.

Meditation

- Make a list of your favorite barbecued foods.
- For each food, consider how it reminds you of God's love, either from the Old Testament Passover story or as a remembrance of Jesus' Last Supper.

Prayer

God of the Passover, you instructed your slavery-bound people to sprinkle the blood of the lamb on their houses and to eat its roasted flesh with unleavened bread and bitter herbs, while you passed over them and set them free. In the fullness of time, you have numbered me among your chosen people and set me free with the blood of your Son, Jesus. Keep me faithful to his teaching, and lead me to the kingdom, where he lives and reigns with you and the Holy Spirit, one God, for ever and ever. Amen.

Honey

Moses hid his face, for he was afraid to look at God. Then the LORD said, "I have observed the misery of my people who are in Egypt; I have heard their cry on account of their taskmasters. Indeed, I know their sufferings, and I have come down to deliver them from the Egyptians, and to bring them up out of that land to a good and broad land, a land flowing with milk and honey" (Exodus 3:6-8).

Reflection

In today's diet-conscious society, more and more of us are discovering the natural sweetness of honey. Instead of sprinkling sugar on our cereal or into our coffee, we substitute a teaspoon of honey.

Honey, the sweet, sticky substance made by bees from the nectar of flowers, is stored and sealed in a honeycomb as food for the bee colony. In biblical times, honey was a delicacy and was considered a sign of abundance.

God promised to free the Israelites from Egyptian slavery and lead them to the land promised to Abraham. In the words of Genesis, this land would be "a good and broad land, a land flowing with milk and honey" (Genesis 3:8).

The Prophet Ezekiel compares the word of God to the sweetness of honey. The voice in Ezekiel's vision tells him to eat the scroll and speak to the house of Israel. The prophet records, "...I ate it; and in my mouth it was as sweet as honey." Then the voice said, "Mortal, go to the house of Israel and speak my very words to them" (Ezekiel 3:3-4).

The Book of Revelation borrows from this image. Handing the visionary a small scroll, the angel says, "Take it and eat; it will be bitter to your stomach, but sweet as honey in your mouth" (Revelation 10:9). The author writes, "...I took the little scroll from the hand of the angel and ate it; it was sweet as honey in my mouth, but when I had eaten it, my stomach was made bitter" (Revelation 10:10).

The word of God is sweet at first. For Moses, it meant liberation; for Ezekiel, confidence; for the visionary, a promise of victory for God's people. But after the sweetness, comes the digesting of the word. For Moses, that entailed leading the yet-to-be-united Israelites out of Egypt—no small task! For Ezekiel, it meant speaking to the Israelites about their exile. For the visionary, it announced the suffering the people would endure before their victory.

Today we hear God's word and devour it, but this calls us to act, to change our way of life. Its sweetness can turn sour as we strive to make the word come alive in our flesh.

Meditation

- Identify five ways that the word of God has sweetened your life.
- Identify five ways that the word of God has called you to change and conversion.

Prayer

God of Moses, Ezekiel, and visionaries, you have spoken your word through your patriarchs, prophets and apostles. Indeed, your word is sweeter than honey from the comb. Enable me to savor its sweetness and endure its sourness as I strive to bring life to your word. I trust in your promise that I shall feast forever on the best of wheat and on honey from the rock of your stability and abundance. I ask this through Jesus Christ, your Son, who lives and reigns with you and the Holy Spirit, one God, for ever and ever. Amen.

Ice

The LORD answered Job out of the whirlwind:
"Who is this that darkens counsel by words without
knowledge?
Gird up your loins like a man, I will question you, and
you shall declare to me.
Where were you when I laid the foundation of the
earth?
Tell me, if you have understanding....
Has the rain a father,
or who has begotten the drops of dew?
From whose womb did the ice come forth,
and who has given birth to the hoarfrost of heaven?
The waters become hard like stone,
and the face of the deep is frozen."

Job 38:1-4, 28-30

Reflection

Ice is one of God's gifts that we most often take for granted. To get a few ice cubes to cool our drinks, we merely have to open the door of our freezer, take out the trays, and turn them upside down. Even before we had electricity and refrigerators, large blocks of ice were delivered to homes by the local ice man. These ice blocks were placed into family iceboxes and used to keep food cool and fresh.

We also use ice for healing our wounds. We can apply it to bruises or aching muscles to bring down swelling or ease pain.

In the far north, large bodies of ice, called glaciers, move down the mountains. As they move, they separate and form icebergs in the ocean. On a bright day, refracted sunlight makes the icebergs look blue.

In some areas of the world, winter brings sleet—tiny frozen drops of rain. At other times, rain freezes into ice as it falls, transforming the world into a crystal fairy land. We stand back and marvel at the beauty of the ice and the powerful presence of its Creator.

Meditation

- Make a list of any natural wonders that lead you to or point you toward God.
- Identify how each of these reveals God to you.

Prayer

God of the cold, you spread your snow like wool, and you strew your frost like ashes. You scatter hail like crumbs. Before you the waters freeze. Winter reveals to me the power of your presence and the warmth of your love. Open my eyes to the beauty of the earth that surrounds me in every season. I ask this through Jesus Christ, your Son, who lives and reigns with you and the Holy Spirit, one God, for ever and ever. Amen.

Icon

[Jesus] is the image of the invisible God, the firstborn of all creation; for in him all things in heaven and on earth were created, things visible and invisible....All things have been created through him and for him. He himself is before all things, and in him all things hold together (Colossians 1:15-17).

Reflection

An icon is a sacred image used for worship. In Christian art, especially in the Eastern Rites, an image of Christ, Mary, or a particular saint is painted on a small wooden panel and used in the liturgy. Icons are reminders of our love and devotion for those whose images they portray.

In our own homes or offices, we display photographs of people we love to remind us of how special they are to us. Somehow the photographs make the person present. Our photo albums are filled with memories of meals shared, trips taken, or special days in our lives.

The Book of Genesis tells us that the first man and woman were made in the image of God, but this image was blurred by sin. The author of the letter to the Colossians explains that Jesus is the image of God. In Jesus, the invisible God becomes visible to us.

When we were baptized, we put on the image of Jesus and we too became images of the invisible God—we became living icons. Now, when we look at our brothers and sisters in

Christ, we are reminded that each person also reflects God's image, and we learn to honor our brothers and sisters as we would honor our God.

Meditation

- What pictures do you have in your home and office?
- Of whom does each remind you?
- Do you have any icons of Jesus, Mary, or the saints in your home and office? What thoughts or feelings do they evoke?
- In your parish church, which icons, statues or pictures are most special to you?

Prayer

Invisible God of creation, on the sixth day of the foundation of the world you created man and woman in your image, but they sinned and blurred the likeness. Through Jesus, your Son, your visible image, the firstborn of all creation, you restored marred human nature. Through the gift of your Holy Spirit, mold me into the image of your Christ that I might be a worthy icon of your love and devotion for the world. Hear my prayer through Jesus, who lives and reigns with you and the Holy Spirit, one God, for ever and ever. Amen.

Jar

Then the word of the Lord came to [Elijah], saying, "Go now to Zarephath, which belongs to Sidon, and live there; for I have commanded a widow there to feed you." So he set out and went to Zarephath. When he came to the gate of the town, a widow was there gathering sticks; he called to her and said, "Bring me a little water in a vessel, so that I may drink." As she was going to bring it, he called to her and said, "Bring me a morsel of bread in your hand." But she said, "As the Lord your God lives, I have nothing baked, only a handful of meal in a jar, and a little oil in a jug; I am now gathering a couple of sticks, so that I may go home and prepare it for myself and my son, that we may eat it, and die." Elijah said to her, "Do not be afraid; go and do as you have said; but first make me a little cake of it and bring it to me, and afterwards make something for yourself and your son. For thus says the Lord the God of Israel: The jar of meal will not be emptied and the jug of oil will not fail until the day that the Lord sends rain on the earth." She went and did as Elijah said, so that she as well as he and her household ate for many days. The jar of meal was not emptied, neither did the jug of oil fail, according to the word of the Lord that he spoke by Elijah (1 Kings 17:8-16).

Reflection

I have two old mason canning jars that belonged to my great-grandmother. Rubber rings on the lids assure a tight seal. At one time, all food was stored and preserved in such jars. Today food is preserved in tin, plastic, ceramic and china. The containers have changed, but the function—storage and preservation of food—remains the same.

In the Scripture passage, the widow's jar of meal and jug of oil meant survival in a time of drought. Through Elijah, God promised that her jar would not go empty and her jug would not run dry. God kept this promise. The widow, her son, and Elijah ate the bread made from the meal and oil for a long time.

There is more to this story than the miracle of the never-ending jar of meal and jug of oil. The widow herself is a type of jar, one filled with the sustaining grace of faith. She trusts the prophet who comes from another land. She is not an Israelite, yet because she is open God fills her with to overflowing with faith.

The same is true for us. God comes to us when we least expect. And, as long as we do not keep our hearts sealed too tightly, God can fill us with a faith that will never run dry.

Meditation

- Think of yourself as a jar. Make a list of the different ways in which God has filled you.
- List occasions when you realize that your heart has been sealed off from God.

Prayer

God of plenty, those who are open to your word discover that their jar of faith never empties or runs dry. Through the words of your Son, Jesus, you fill me with grace, as once you filled the jar of the widow of Zarephath with meal. Remove all that hinders me from being open to the fullness of your presence this day. I ask this through Jesus Christ, who lives and reigns with you and the Holy Spirit, one God, for ever and ever. Amen.

Keys

*Thus says the Lord God of hosts: Come, go to this
steward, to Shebna, who is master of the household, and
say to him:...The Lord is about to hurl you away vio-
lently, my fellow....I will thrust you from your office, and
you will be pulled down from your post. On that day I
will call my servant, Eliakim son of Hilkiah, and will
clothe him with your robe, and bind your sash on him. I
will commit your authority to his hand, and he shall be a
father to the inhabitants of Jerusalem and to the house of
Judah. I will place on his shoulder the key of the house
of David; he shall open, and no one shall shut; he shall
shut, and no one shall open (Isaiah 22:15, 17, 19-22).*

Reflection

I carry fourteen keys on my key chain: three car keys—
two to one car and one to another; three house keys—two to
the front door and one to the back; two university office
keys—one to my office there and one to the mail room; two
keys to The Catholic Center—one to the main door and one
to my office there; two door keys to the home of a friend; a
safety deposit box key; and the key to my desk at home. I
also keep keys in a box in my desk that open my filing cabinet, luggage, briefcase, bicycle lock, trunk and computer. If
I didn't tag each key, I'd probably forget what each one
opened.

In biblical times, a key was a sign of authority. Locks
were huge and the key had to be carried over the shoulder
of the master of the palace. It took so long to lock and
unlock the door that, once closed and locked in the evening,
it stayed that way until morning .

In Matthew's Gospel, Jesus uses the symbol of the key to entrust the care of the church to Peter and the apostles: "I will give you the keys of the kingdom of heaven, and whatever you bind on earth will be bound in heaven, and whatever you loose on earth will be loosed in heaven" (Matthew 16:19).

The Book of Revelation uses the same imagery to indicate that Jesus, through his suffering, death and resurrection, has supreme authority over the new Jerusalem. The visionary is told to write to the church in Philadelphia: "I know your works. Look, I have set before you an open door, which no one is able to shut. I know that you have but little power, and yet you have kept my word and have not denied my name" (Revelation 3:7-8).

Even today, keys symbolize authority. A key to the office building means we have authority to enter there. When a teenager gets a driver's license, parents may hand over a set of keys to the car, showing their belief that he or she is ready to accept responsibility.

Meditation

- List the purpose of each key on your key chain. Do the same with the keys in your desk, bureau or cabinet.
- Identify what authority and power each key gives you.

Prayer

God of David, you entrusted the key to the king's palace to one who would exercise his authority and power with care. You sent your Son and entrusted to him the key to salvation He, in turn, entrusted to his apostles the keys to your kingdom. Help me to exercise the authority entrusted to me with care and to use my power to further the kingdom, where you live and reign with your Son, Jesus Christ, and the Holy Spirit, one God, for ever and ever. Amen.

Lamp

[Jesus said,] "No one after lighting a lamp puts it in a cellar, but on the lamp stand so that those who enter may see the light. Your eye is the lamp of your body. If your eye is healthy, your whole body is full of light; but if it is not healthy, your body is full of darkness. Therefore consider whether the light in you is not darkness. If then your whole body is full of light, with no part of it in darkness, it will be as full of light as when a lamp gives you light with its rays" (Luke 11:33-36).

Reflection

When we hear the word "lamp," we usually think of a decorative stand with a bulb screwed into its top and a shade over the bulb. A simple flick of the switch or touch of the lamp will cause the bulb to shed artificial light throughout a room.

It was not this way for my great-grandmother, however. For her, the word "lamp" indicated a clear glass container with a cotton wick dipping into dark yellow fuel on one end and topped with a chimney. This was great-grandmother's "coal oil lamp."

In the evening, when the last streak of light had faded from the sky, great-grandmother would strike a wooden Diamond match against the emery board on the side of the box and set the lamp ablaze. I would enjoy watching its shadows dancing on the walls as people moved around the room. The lamp was always placed in a prominent location: the middle of the table for dinner or on a shelf in the living room for the rest of the evening.

There was something natural and authentic about my great-grandmother's coal oil lamp. We were drawn to its softness as the family gathered around it. The coal oil lamp provided a security zone for sharing—something an electric light bulb cannot do. Conversation and prayer blossomed in its glow.

Even after electricity was installed in great-grandmother's home, she kept her coal oil lamp. Winter and summer, she would light it in the evening, preferring its warmth and its soft, somber, reflective atmosphere to the glare of the electric lights. Today, I remember her each time I turn off my lights, strike a match, and light a candle. The soft light and the dancing shadows prepare my thoughts for intimate prayer.

As Christians, we are called to be lamps burning brightly with the Good News of Jesus. No one can hide our enthusiasm for the poor, our hours of volunteer work, our love for family and friends. Our light draws others to Jesus, who is the fuel that keeps our lights aglow.

Meditation

- Make a list of ways you can be a person of light, a lamp for others.
- Which of these do you think is the most important?
- Whose darkness have you scattered with the light from your lamp?

Prayer

God of light, in you there is no darkness. Down through the ages, you have spoken your word to your people through your patriarchs and matriarchs, prophets and prophetesses, kings and queens. You have given me Jesus, your Son, your eternal Word, who is the light of the world. May his teaching be a lamp for my feet, a light that guides me in his paths to the kingdom, where he lives and reigns with you and the Holy Spirit, one God, for ever and ever. Amen.

Mailbox

This is the message we have heard from him and pro-
claim to you, that God is light and in him there is no
darkness at all. If we say that we have fellowship with
him while we are walking in darkness, we lie and do not
do what is true; but if we walk in the light as he himself
is in the light, we have fellowship with one another, and
the blood of Jesus his Son cleanses us from all sin
(1 John 1:5-7).

Reflection

An important item for every home is the mailbox. For some, this is a rented box at the Post Office; for others it means delivery right to our door of messages and words of greeting.

When I get home in the evening, the first thing I do is flip through the mail to find the personal items—a letter from a family member, a greeting card from a friend, even bills that must be dealt with as soon as possible.

Into our mailboxes we place letters crafted with care that we send to our friends. At Christmas time, we look to our mailboxes for greetings from people we haven't heard from in a year; and we return our greetings to them. From our own mailboxes, we send messages around the world; from the mailboxes of others, we receive responses.

From God's perspective, the world is a mailbox. God's word and God's message to us became flesh in the person of God's only Son, Jesus, who taught us to walk in God's light, to act in God's truth, and to have fellowship with one another. We can act in truth by following Jesus' teaching in the Bible. We have fellowship with one another by being honest with each other and treating each other with respect.

To receive God's word, we must be ready to accept the message, excited about reading it, and open to the Good News God sends us. God never sends junk mail, addressed to "Resident," to be tossed away without being opened. The Bible, God's message to us, is a love letter to be savored and answered by following the loving way of the messenger who is also the message—Jesus.

Meditation

- Take your Bible to a quiet place in your home where you can sit and relax. Open to any place, choose a few verses, and read them slowly and carefully.
- What message are you getting from God?
- How can you answer God's letter to you by living it today?

Prayer

Eternal God, in the past you spoke your word in partial and various ways to my ancestors through the prophets. Now you have spoken to me through your only-begotten Son, Jesus. Open my ears that I may hear your word; open my mind that I may understand your message; open my heart that I may receive your letter of love with delight. Hear my prayer through Jesus Christ, who lives and reigns with you and the Holy Spirit, one God, for ever and ever. Amen.

Mirror

We know only in part, and we prophesy only in part; but when the complete comes, the partial will come to an end. When I was a child, I spoke like a child, I thought like a child, I reasoned like a child; when I became an adult, I put an end to childish ways. For now we see in a mirror, dimly, but then we will see face to face. Now I know only in part; than I will know fully, even as I have been fully known (1 Corinthians 13:9-12).

Reflection

In most homes, there's a mirror on the front door of the medicine cabinet, a mirror attached to the dresser, and a mirror beside the front door where we can check our appearance before presenting ourselves to others. We use mirrors to comb our hair, to shave, or to put on make-up. We see ourselves reflected over and over. We know exactly what we look like, warts and all!

As children we loved to stand in front of a mirror making silly faces. As we grew older, we examined our blossoming bodies in front of the mirror. We practiced our lines for the school play before a mirror. Some people use mirrors to practice a speech before facing a live audience.

Today, mirrors are made of glass backed with quicksilver or foil to reflect images. In biblical times, mirrors were made from polished metal; the reflected image was blurred or dim. If we look at ourselves in the aluminum side of a toaster or coffee pot, we can see how difficult it must have been to get an accurate image.

While today's mirrors enable us to see ourselves exactly as we are physically, they do not provide a full picture of who we really are. This fuller image is seen only by God. We live with this imperfection now, but one day all that God has made us to be and all that we have made of ourselves will be revealed. And we shall know God as fully as God already knows us. Our mirrors can remind us daily that what we see is but a dim reflection of what we will become in God's presence.

Meditation

- Stand in front of a mirror and look at yourself.
- List the gifts God has given to you—those you can see and those you know.
- For each gift identify a way you can make better use of it by reflecting it to others.

Prayer

Hidden God, you refused to reveal your face to Moses, but you did show us your image in the person of your only-begotten Son, Jesus. Since you have created me in your image and likeness, I have come to realize that my dim reflection in a mirror is but a glimpse of your possibilities, as seen in the faces of your many people. Guide me to the fullness of what you have created me to be through Jesus Christ, who lives and reigns with you and the Holy Spirit, one God, for ever and ever. Amen.

Name

But now thus says the LORD,
  he who created you, O Jacob,
  he who formed you, O Israel:
Do not fear, for I have redeemed you;
  I have called you by name, you are mine.
When you pass through the waters, I will be with you;
  and through the rivers, they shall not overwhelm you;
  when you walk through fire you shall not be burned,
  and the flame shall not consume you.
For I am the LORD your God,
  the Holy One of Israel, your Savior.

Isaiah 43:1-3

Reflection

One of the first gifts we receive is our name. It identifies who we are and distinguishes us from everyone else. We use our names to mark our possessions: name tags sewn into clothing, name plates or seals pasted in our books, tags on our luggage. The name on our driver's license proves to others that we are who we say we are. Our names appear on personal stationery and note pads.

We have a God who is personal enough, near enough, loving enough to call us each by name. And God told Moses, "I am Who I am....This is my name forever, and this my title for all generations" (Exodus 3:14, 15). This name identifies God as the very essence of being.

Jesus told us to call God "Abba" (Father or Daddy), a term of endearment that indicates how deeply God loves people, redeems them, and saves them. God's name is also

"Mother." The prophet Isaiah compares the great city, Jerusalem, where God was believed to live in the temple with his people, to a woman who has just given birth. "Rejoice with Jerusalem, and be glad for her," states the prophet, "that you may nurse and be satisfied from her consoling breast; that you may drink deeply with delight from her glorious bosom." The prophet continues his comparison, "You shall nurse and be carried on her arm, and dandled on her knees" (Isaiah 66:10-12). God called us by name, gave us life, and feeds us daily, just as our mother gave us life and nourished us with milk from her breasts. Mother or Father, Yahweh or Lord, our God knows us, loves us, and calls us by name.

Meditation

- Walk through your home and list the places where you find your name.
- After each item on your list, indicate what it reveals about you.
- What names do you use in reference to God? What do these names tell you about your relationship with God? What do they say about you?

Prayer

From the rising to the setting of the sun may your name be praised, almighty God, for there is no name more glorious in all the earth than yours. I sing praise to your name as Lord and King and Savior. I place my trust in your name as Father and Mother. Keep me near to you as a child to a parent. I ask this in the name of Jesus Christ, your Son, who lives and reigns with you and the Holy Spirit, one God, for ever and ever. Amen.

Ottoman

My brothers and sisters, do you with your acts of favoritism really believe in our glorious Lord Jesus Christ? For if a person with gold rings and in fine clothes comes into your assembly, and if a poor person in dirty clothes also comes in, and if you take notice of the one wearing the fine clothes and say, "Have a seat here, please," while to the one who is poor you say, "Stand there," or "Sit at my feet," have you not made distinctions among yourselves, and become judges with evil thoughts? (James 2:1-4).

Reflection

An ottoman is a footrest or footstool. Some are fancy, some are plain; some are upholstered to match a chair or sofa; some are simple wooden stools; others are large enough to hold feet, the Sunday paper, and a pizza. Today, many recliners come with built-in ottomans. Pull a handle located alongside the chair and a footstool pops up.

It doesn't take much thinking to determine that, given a choice, we'd rather sit in the chair than on the ottoman, which has no backrest. We wouldn't dream of asking a special guest to sit on a footstool when a chair is available.

In biblical times, the more important guests sat closer to the host, while those of lesser importance were told to sit farther away or on a stool at the host's feet. Saint James addresses this issue and makes it clear that, in the Christian community, all people are equal; no one is more important than anyone else. We cannot give a lower place to someone because he or she is of a different sex, creed, color or ethnic background. In God's eyes, no one sits on a footstool— there are no ottomans, only very important chairs!

This is a Christian view which our society does not always recognize. Think about it. Why does it take a federal law to bring whites, blacks, and other races of students together for school? Why, in some neighborhoods, can't certain people buy a home because they happen to have the wrong color of skin? And why does our attire influence some employers more than our resumés?

Jesus treats all God's people as equals. No one is any less or greater in his eyes. In Jesus' world, like in God's, there are no ottomans—only chairs!

Meditation

- Identify ways you place people on footstools in your thoughts, in your heart, in your home, around your table.
- Identify ways you can treat these and all human beings with equal dignity.

Prayer

God, you have no equal, but you dwell in a perfect Trinity of three equal persons. Around your banquet table, all places are seats of honor and dignity. Guide my thoughts and change my heart so I may look upon and treat all of your children with the equal human dignity with which you endowed them. I make this prayer in the name of Jesus Christ, your Son, who lives and reigns with you, Father, and the Holy Spirit, one God, for ever and ever. Amen.

Oven

When I would restore the fortunes of my people,
when I would heal Israel,
the corruption of Ephraim is revealed,
and the wicked deeds of Samaria....
By their wickedness they make the king glad,
and the officials by their treachery.
They are all adulterers;
they are like a heated oven,
whose baker does not need to stir the fire,
from the kneading of the dough until it is
leavened.

Hosea 7:1, 3-4

Reflection

Today, most homes have a conventional oven built into their range, plus a separate microwave oven usually located on a counter top. When we think of conventional ovens, we think about baking breads, cakes and pies; roasting turkeys, cuts of beef, and shanks of pork; cooking casseroles; and warming rolls. Most people use their microwave ovens to prepare simple dishes or warm up leftovers.

I remember my great-grandmother's wood-burning cook stove. When preparing any item in the oven, she'd ask me to watch the temperature gauge that was built into the oven door. A few sticks of wood would make the oven hotter; less wood allowed it to cool. Keeping an even temperature was no small task. Often, food was either overcooked or under done!

We can compare the heat of an oven to our anger or wrath. We might find ourselves getting hot over a disagreement at home or at work or flare up over having to perform a job we do not like. At times, we can even reach the boiling point and strike out randomly at anyone who happens to cross our tracks.

But we can also view our oven as a holy symbol. As we bake, roast, broil and cook our food, the heat of the oven kills harmful bacteria and other toxic substances. From the fruits of our ovens, we spread a table for family and friends. The old Pillsbury commercial captures a bit of truth: "Nothin' says lovin' like somethin' from the oven!"

Meditation

- How does your anger resemble your oven? List ways you can regulate the heat that comes from your anger.
- During the past month, list those who have shared the riches of your oven.
- Indicate how you are related to each person on your list.

Prayer

God of the kitchen, you have taught me that a place is set for me at your heavenly banquet table. When I call family and friends to my table to share the riches from my oven, make me aware of how wide is the circle to which you invite all people. May the smells of baking, roasting, broiling and cooking, which waft through the air from my oven, remind me of the eternal feast to be shared with you, Father, your Son, Jesus Christ, and the Holy Spirit, who live and reign as one God, for ever and ever. Amen.

Pillow

[Jacob] came to a certain place and stayed there for the night, because the sun had set. Taking one of the stones of the place, he put it under his head and lay down in that place. And he dreamed that there was a ladder set up on the earth, the top of it reaching to heaven; and the angels of God were ascending and descending on it.

And he was afraid, and said, "How awesome is this place! This is none other than the house of God, and this is the gate of heaven." So Jacob rose early in the morning, and he took the stone that he had put under his head and set it up for a pillar and poured oil on top of it (Genesis 28:11-12, 16-18).

Reflection

When we think of a pillow, most of us picture a soft, downy support for our heads at night. But there are other kinds of pillows around our homes. A small pillow on a couch or chair can be used to support a person's back. A pillow next to my own favorite chair gives me something to lean my head against should I decide to fall asleep! Large throw pillows on the floor are great to sit or sprawl on, especially for children watching television.

Pillows of varying shapes and sizes serve as decorations for a bed or a sofa; some are embroidered or bordered in lace. The ring bearer at a wedding carries the rings of the bride and groom on a pillow shaped like a heart.

Whatever the size or style, a pillow is basically a cloth bag filled with feathers, down, sponge rubber or plastic fiber. It's hard to imagine using a stone for a pillow, yet when

Jacob was tired, he rested his head on a stone and slept. In his dream, God's presence was made known to him. Jacob then used his stone pillow as a place marker so the people would always remember that God was with them there.

Throughout the Bible, God's presence is made known through dreams. Jacob's son, Joseph, was a dreamer—and a vehicle for God's revelation. Young Samuel was called by God while he slept. God directed Joseph, Mary's espoused, to take her as his wife, though she was already with child. After the birth of Jesus, God cautioned Joseph to take the child and his mother to Egypt to escape the wrath of Herod. God directed the Magi through a dream not to return to Herod.

We too can be directed by God through our dreams as we sleep soundly on our pillows. A good night's sleep can give us a new perspective on an old problem. The prayer on our lips as we fall asleep often returns to our thoughts in the morning. A quick afternoon nap on our favorite pillow can help us sort through what God asks of us each day.

Meditation

- Walk through your home and list the places and uses of the pillows you find.
- For each pillow, identify how it might be seen as a shrine, a spot where God is found.
- For each place, can you remember a time when God was revealed to you there?

Prayer

Lord God, you reveal yourself and your will for your people through their dreams as they rest their heads upon pillows. In times of distress, when I stain my pillow with tears, awaken me to the realization that your presence makes my bed, sofa or chair a holy place. Father, make my home a shrine in which you dwell with your Son, Jesus Christ, and the Holy Spirit, one God, for ever and ever. Amen.

Quilt

A capable wife who can find?
She is far more precious than jewels.
The heart of her husband trusts in her,
and he will have no lack of gain.
She is not afraid for her household when it snows,
for all her household are clothed in crimson.
She makes herself coverings;
her clothing is fine linen and purple.

Proverbs 31:10-11, 21-22

Reflection

A quilt is a covering made from two layers of cloth stuffed with wool, cotton or down and stitched together in a decorative design or tacked evenly with a heavy thread. I have three quilts that are especially important to me. All were crafted by hand, a long and tedious process called "quilting." Two were made by relatives of my great-grandmother and passed on to me; the third was made especially for me by my "second mother," an aunt with whom I spent almost six of my teenage years. When I use these quilts, they flood my mind with memories.

Before blankets became common, quilts had a practical purpose. They were used on beds for warmth. Today, we more often use them as decorations placed at the foot of the bed or hang them on our walls. Because quilting is an art form, old quilts are often displayed in museums to show the intricacies of their designs.

A quilt can commemorate a special event. A group celebrating a centennial might make a quilt composed of blocks depicting events of its common history. Recently, a large quilt was designed in memory of those who died with AIDS. Panels naming the victims were stitched by loving friends and family members. This quilt tours the country to be displayed in museums and arenas for public viewing.

As we snuggle down under our quilts, memories of God's care and concern for us are unleashed. God warms us with love, pieces together the various dimensions of our lives, keeps us secure, calms us when we are afraid, and covers our failures and shortcomings.

Meditation

- List the quilts you have in your home now or can recall from your childhood.
- Are there special memories associated with these quilts?
- For each person or memory, identify how God was present or involved.

Prayer

God of all, you cover the heavens with clouds and blanket the earth with food for people and animals. When Israel escaped Egyptian slavery, you spread your quilt of fire during the night and your quilt of cloud during the day to protect your people. Cover me with your love. I remember your great deeds of the past and look forward anxiously to even greater ones in the future. I ask this through Jesus Christ, your Son, who lives and reigns with you, Father, and the Holy Spirit, one God, for ever and ever. Amen.

Refrigerator

Listen, listen to the thunder of [God's] voice
and the rumbling that comes from his mouth.
Under the whole heaven he lets it loose,
and his lightning to the corners of the earth....
From its chamber comes the whirlwind,
and cold from the scattering winds.
By the breath of God ice is given,
and the broad waters are frozen fast.

Job 37:2-3, 9-10

Reflection

For years, I owned a small refrigerator with a drawer for fruits and vegetables, two shelves about eight inches apart, and a freezer large enough for two trays for ice cubes. It did not hold much food. In winter, I kept perishables in my garage...my "outside refrigerator."

A few of us may remember iceboxes, those wooden cabinets that held large blocks of ice and our perishables. When the ice melted, we were left with a pool of water on the floor!

Modern refrigerators self-defrost and make ice cubes automatically. In restaurants and butcher shops, refrigerators can be as large as a room. Whatever their shape, dimension or use, refrigerators continue to preserve our perishable food items.

Ancient peoples stood in awe and wonder at the change of seasons and the coming of wintertime. They felt the cold on their skins and saw the frost on the grass and the trees; they walked over the frozen streams and rivers. Since they could not harness the cold, they worshiped God as the source and regulator of this unexplainable mystery.

If we live where the seasons change, we experience that same awe and reverence. The cold penetrates our heavy winter clothing, and we shiver as the meteorologist announces the windchill factor. Sparkling hoarfrost on grass and barren branches turns our world into a winter wonderland. We ski, sled and hike in a snow-blanketed playground. Ice-covered ponds become skating rinks, and children and adults glide in a Currier and Ives tableau.

If we live in an area where winter does not freeze over, our refrigerators can be a way to touch the God of the seasons. As we open the door, cold air rushes out and we are momentarily refreshed by the artificial cold, revealing the power of the Creator.

Meditation

- Open your refrigerator door and feel the cold air rush out. List five items you find within your refrigerator.
- For each item, compose a prayer of thanksgiving for God's creation of cold and ice.

Prayer

God of hoarfrost, snow and ice, you strew frost like ashes, you spread snow like wool, and before your cold the waters freeze. In your wisdom you have given the changes of seasons to the earth, so that all people might stand in wonder at your greatness. I lift up my voice in thanksgiving to you for your many manifestations of cold and coolness. Hear my praise, Father, through Jesus Christ, your Son, who lives and reigns with you and the Holy Spirit, one God, for ever and ever. Amen.

Robe

I will greatly rejoice in the Lord,
my whole being shall exult in my God;
for he has clothed me with the garments of salvation,
he has covered me with the robe of righteousness,
as a bridegroom decks himself with a garland,
and as a bride adorns herself with her jewels.
Isaiah 61:10

Reflection

There is something really comforting about our favorite bathrobe. In the evening, after we get dressed for bed, we put it on to watch a little television or curl up with a good book. First thing in the morning, we reach for it as we rise to meet a new day. The robe keeps us warm as we make our way to the kitchen to put on the coffee, and then to the bathroom to shower. As we step out of the shower, we reach again for the robe to cover our nakedness.

Bathrobes come in all types and sizes. Most of them have pockets; some are knee-length; others are floor-length. My favorite robe is a caftan, a cotton, ankle-length garment with long sleeves and a hood. It's warm and cozy on a cold winter's night and a delight to put on after a hot shower.

Getting wrapped in a robe can remind us of how God wraps us in salvation by loving us, saving us, and calling us to be persons of justice. God's love brought us to our birth; God's promise brings us to a new birth in eternity; and God's call challenges us to be persons of justice—not like the blindfolded lady holding scales, but as persons who know what must be done and who must do it.

Meditation

- Put on your favorite robe. List ways you have experienced God's love in the past three days.
- List any deeds of justice you performed in the past three days. Who were the beneficiaries of your just acts?

Prayer

God of love and justice, your robe is our light as you walk on the floor of the clouds and wrap your people in salvation. Before I was a thought, you loved me into being and called me to do justice in your sight. Give me the gift of discernment to know your will and the courage to put it into practice. Hear my prayer through Jesus Christ, your Son, who lives and reigns with you and the Holy Spirit, one God, for ever and ever. Amen.

Shower

We acknowledge our wickedness, O L<small>ORD</small>,
the iniquity of our ancestors,
for we have sinned against you.
Do not spurn us, for your name's sake;
do not dishonor your glorious throne;
remember and do not break your
covenant with us.
Can any idols of the nations bring rain?
Or can the heavens give showers?
Is it not you, O L<small>ORD</small> our God?
We set our hope on you,
for it is you who do all this.

Jeremiah 14:20-22

Reflection

The people of the ancient world imagined the earth as a giant terrarium, supported by columns. Its flat, plate-like surface was bordered by mountains. Across the top was a crescent-shaped dome into which were inserted floodgates. When rain fell upon the earth, it was because God, who lived above the dome, opened the floodgates.

To our enlightened society, a shower is a natural event. In winter, waters from the heavens replenish the dormant earth. In spring, gentle showers nourish the new growth on tree branches and make the flowers bloom. In summer, the thirsty ground aches for heavy rain. Autumn showers soften dead leaves, fostering the decaying process.

One of the first things most of us do in the morning is hop in the shower. We stand in the spray of water and let the dust of yesterday and the sleep of the just-finished night wash away. A morning shower cleanses us and soothes our muscles, preparing us to face the day.

Both the rain from the heavens and our own morning shower can remind us of the day of our baptism, when sin was washed away and we were cleansed and reborn. We were initiated into God's new covenant, established through Jesus. Every shower has the potential to awaken us to the memory of God's promise and to question how well we live our own baptismal promises each day.

Meditation

- List the ways the showers of nature remind you of your baptism.
- List the ways your morning shower can be a daily recommitment to your baptismal covenant.

Prayer

God of heaven and earth, you visit the land and water it, enriching its rivers, drenching its furrows, breaking up its clods, and softening it with showers. When I was dry in sin, you sent your Son, Jesus, who was like rain coming down on the meadow, like a shower watering the earth. With the shower of his blood from the cross he has removed my sin and dressed me in the white garment of your grace. Keep me faithful to the promises of my baptism and guide me to the kingdom, where you live and reign with Jesus and the Holy Spirit, one God, for ever and ever. Amen.

Steps

The human mind plans the way,
but the LORD directs the steps.

Proverbs 16:9

Reflection

With a camera or video recorder in hand, parents capture the first steps of their child. Once the child learns to walk, the world will never be the same. Tiny footsteps will lead the child from the nursery to the bathroom, the kitchen and the family room, each of which contains a world as yet undiscovered.

Each morning, as I hop out of bed, I take my own first steps into a new day and repeat a lesson I learned many years ago. The life I walk into consists of a world waiting to be known, savored and enjoyed. No one will take my photograph or capture my action on video tape, but the first steps of a new day can be as exciting as the first steps of life.

As we learn the balance required to take more than one step at a time, we gradually grow into walking up and down stairs, a series of steps. Some homes contain only a step or two; others may have a staircase leading to another floor. It takes a toddler some time to master the technique required to ascend or descend a stairway safely.

We often think we are in charge of our lives. After all, if we can walk, we can direct our own course. We are in charge of where we put our feet and where our mobility takes us. We don't have to spend a lot of time thinking about getting from one room to another; we just place one foot in front of the other and take our steps—unconsciously.

In truth, it is God who directs our steps, working through us to get us to go where we need to be. Every step we take can spark our awareness of how God inspires us through family and friends and various events. By calling us to step outside, a member of the family can point out the beauty of a sunset. A friend can invite us to step out for an evening of entertainment. By stepping into the world of travel, we can wonder at the wisdom of the Creator in the diversity of peoples, languages, customs and lands. Yes, every step can deepen our awareness of God, who walks by our side with every step we take.

Meditation

- Retrace the steps you took yesterday (or today, if it is afternoon or evening). Identify any people or events that led you to where you might not have gone on your own.
- For each of these, identify how you became aware of God's presence.

Prayer

Almighty God, without my knowing it you guide my steps in your pathways and reveal your wisdom and presence in my life. When my steps falter and I lose my balance and slip, help me to stand again. Do not permit me to turn aside from your ways, but steady my steps according to your promise. Enable me to follow in the footsteps of Jesus, your Son, who lives and reigns with you and the Holy Spirit, one God, for ever and ever. Amen.

Table

Two of [the disciples] were going to a village called Emmaus, about seven miles from Jerusalem, and talking with each other about all these things that had happened. While they were talking and discussing, Jesus himself came near and went with them, but their eyes were kept from recognizing him.

As they came near the village to which they were going, he walked ahead as if he were going on. But they urged him strongly, saying, "Stay with us, because it is almost evening and the day is now nearly over." So he went in to stay with them. When he was at the table with them, he took bread, blessed and broke it, and gave it to them. Then their eyes were opened, and they recognized him; and he vanished from their sight (Luke 24:13-16, 28-31).

Reflection

The family table is a place to recognize each member's unique identity and dignity. As we dine with our loved ones, we get to know each other, share our pain, solve problems, and get direction. As bread is broken and shared, as glasses are lifted in a toast, we tell our stories, drinking deeply of one another and discovering God in our midst.

We gather for meals with family and friends. We do not invite strangers or enemies to sit and eat with us! Carefully prepared foods are passed around, and we dish out our portions. Besides sharing food, we share our day's activities. To adapt an old cliché, the family that eats together stays together.

Fast food institutions have taken a toll on family intimacy, but on special occasions such as Thanksgiving, Christmas, Easter, and often on Sunday afternoons, family and friends still gather around the table for a meal. These are special times, but we also need to take time during the week to share our lives through listening and speaking, to drink of the wealth of experiences of everyone at the table.

In some cultures, an extra place is set at the table for God. To invite God to our table is to recognize the divine presence in our midst. As we share food and drink and companionship, God's presence is revealed to us through one another.

As at Emmaus, however, as soon as we recognize this fact, God disappears, calling us to delve even more deeply into the mystery of the loved ones who join us at table.

Meditation

- Recall three recent meals around your table. Who was there for each meal?
- Identify how God was revealed through your sharing of food, drink and life.

Prayer

O Lord, my God, you spread the table of your grace through the people who gather to dine at my table. Through food and drink, you open my eyes to the unique dignity of every human person and teach me to respect all of your creation. Help me to recognize your presence in every person who joins me at my table. As we share our lives, may I taste of and see your goodness until I come to the eternal banquet table in the kingdom, where you live with Jesus Christ, your Son, and the Holy Spirit, one God, for ever and ever. Amen.

Toilet Bowl

[Jesus] called the crowd again and said to them, "Listen to me, all of you, and understand: there is nothing outside a person that by going in can defile, but the things that come out are what defile."

When he had left the crowd and entered the house, his disciples asked him about the parable. He said to them, "Then do you also fail to understand? Do you not see that whatever goes into a person from outside cannot defile, since it enters, not the heart but the stomach, and goes out into the sewer?" (Thus he declared all foods clean.) And he said, "It is what comes out of a person that defiles. For it is from within, from the human heart, that evil intentions come: fornication, theft, murder, adultery, avarice, wickedness, deceit, licentiousness, envy, slander, pride, folly. All these evil things come from within, and they defile a person" (Mark 7:14-15, 17-23).

Reflection

The least-liked task in every home is cleaning the toilet bowl. Even with the new drop-in tank cleaners, deodorizers, whiteners and crystals, eventually we must take a brush and scrub the bowl.

I grew up without indoor plumbing. Until I was eight or nine, the "toilet bowl" was the outhouse, a primitive building located about a hundred yards behind my family's home. It was hot and smelly in the summer and cold and snappy in the winter. But it had one advantage over the toilet bowl—it never had to be cleaned!

All of us make daily visits to the toilet bowl to relieve our bodies of solid wastes and liquid poisons, the results of our body's interior self-cleaning. With the push of a handle, a few gallons of water wash away all that can be harmful to us and to others.

Some people refer to their toilet bowl as a throne; and in some homes, that is what it seems to be. Scattered on the floor around it are magazines, books and newspapers. There may be an ashtray for smokers as well as a place to set a coffee mug.

What an ideal place to think about God! Where else can we find such solitude and quiet? Where else can we come to realize the truth of our Scripture passage that it is not what we eat that defiles us, but the sin that emerges from our hearts? As we contemplate and recognize our sin, we can eliminate it and flush it away with the rest of our waste.

Meditation

- Inspire bathroom meditation by setting out a candle, a Bible, a religious magazine or book, and a short prayer on a plaque.
- Whenever you use your toilet bowl, ask yourself, "What waste needs to be eliminated from my heart?"

Prayer

Cleansing God, you know the innermost secrets of my heart and you continually call me to repentance and change. Give me the courage to face what comes from within, so that with your help I might eliminate sin from my life. Washed in the blood of your Son, Jesus, enable me to grow in love for you, for all your people, and for all of your creation. I ask this through Jesus Christ, who lives and reigns with you and the Holy Spirit, one God, for ever and ever. Amen.

Umbrella

Jonah went out of the city [of Nineveh] and sat down east of the city, and made a booth for himself there. He sat under it in the shade, waiting to see what would become of the city.

The LORD God appointed a bush, and made it come up over Jonah, to give shade over his head, to save him from his discomfort; so Jonah was very happy about the bush. But when dawn came up the next day, God appointed a worm that attacked the bush, so that it withered. When the sun arose, God prepared a sultry east wind, and the sun beat down on the head of Jonah so that he was faint and asked that he might die. He said, "It is better for me to die than to live."

But God said to Jonah, "Is it right for you to be angry about the bush?" And he said, "Yes, angry enough to die." Then the LORD said, "You are concerned about the bush, for which you did not labor and which you did not grow; it came into being in a night and perished in a night. And should I not be concerned about Nineveh, that great city, in which there are more than a hundred and twenty thousand persons who do not know their right hand from their left, and also many animals?" (Jonah 4:5-11).

Reflection

On rainy days, umbrellas sprout like mushrooms. All of us own at least one. We may have a large, cane-handle type or a collapsible one that fits into our briefcase or book-pack. Whatever our style, our umbrellas keep us dry when it rains.

We also find umbrellas on the beach, where people huddle under them for a reprieve from the sun. Long ago, women carried "parasols" as accessories to their daily dress. These too were used as protection from the sun.

We store our umbrellas in a stand in our foyer, near the back door, in a closet, or under the seat of our cars. Because they are used for protection from the rain, sun and snow, we leave them where they will always be easy to grab and use.

Our umbrellas can remind us of God's sheltering protection. We recognize God's concern for all people (and animals) in our Scripture passage from the book of the prophet Jonah. God's love covers us and shelters us like an umbrella in all kinds of weather.

Meditation

- Find an umbrella and open it over you. Identify three recent experiences you have had of God's protection, mercy, concern or care for you.

Prayer

God of rain, sun and snow, from the rising of the sun to its setting your name is deserving of praise. Father, you guard me with your mercy so that the rain may not cause my feet to slip. Your concern for me protects me from the sun in the heat of the day. Your care for me is like a blanket of freshly fallen snow. Be with me in my coming and in my going. Hear my prayer through Jesus Christ, your Son, who lives and reigns with you and the Holy Spirit, one God, for ever and ever. Amen.

Vacuum

[Jesus said,] "...What woman having ten silver coins, if she loses one of them, does not light a lamp, sweep the house, and search carefully until she finds it? When she has found it, she calls together her friends and neighbors, saying, 'Rejoice with me, for I have found the coin that I lost.' Just so, I tell you, there is joy in the presence of the angels of God over one sinner who repents" (Luke 15:8-10).

Reflection

A vacuum is a space devoid of matter, an emptiness. Our vacuum cleaner or sweeper cleans our carpets, furniture, drapes and floors by sucking the dust and dirt into a bag for disposal.

My vacuum cleaner sits in the closet near my front door. When I need to do a quick clean-up, I roll it out, plug it in, and in a few minutes the dirt is gone. For small jobs I own a hand-held vacuum to gobble up the spills and crumbs.

My great-grandmother used to sweep her floors with a homemade broom. Every year she'd plant a few rows of broomcorn, a cultivated sorghum whose stiff-branched flower clusters (panicles) were used to make brooms. She'd harvest the panicles, gather them together around a handle, and tie them tightly with a cord. The result was the birth of a new broom.

We still use "store-bought" brooms, as my great-grandmother called them, to clean tile and linoleum floors. We sweep the dirt into a pile, push it into a dustpan, and empty it in the trash. We use brooms outside to sweep new-mown grass off of the sidewalk in the summer and snow from our path in the winter. A broom is also handy for sweeping the concrete floors of our garages and basements.

Whether we sweep with a broom or clean with a vacuum, it has the same effect—we create a dirt-free space. With this understanding, we can see how our vacuums can inspire us to recall the God who removes our imperfections and creates a sin-free space where the Holy Spirit can dwell.

Like a woman with a great broom on spring-cleaning day, God sweeps through our lives, searching through the dust of sin until we are found and cleansed. We praise the God who overwhelms evil with love to create this occasion of joy!

Meditation

- Identify three times in your life when the house of your soul was dusty with sin and God found you and forgave you.
- For each of these, compose a short prayer of thanksgiving.

Prayer

God of forgiveness, you have cleansed me of sin through the blood of your Son, Jesus, and you have washed me and made me whiter than snow through the waters of baptism. Continue to give me the grace of repentance. Make my hands sinless. Make my heart clean. Make me not desire what is vain. Enable me to praise you for your gift of overwhelming love, which was displayed on the cross through Jesus Christ, who lives and reigns with you and the Holy Spirit, one God, for ever and ever. Amen.

Walls

In the spirit [the angel] carried me away to a great, high mountain and showed me the holy city Jerusalem coming down out of heaven from God. It has the glory of God and a radiance like a very rare jewel, like jasper, clear as crystal. It has a great, high wall with twelve gates, and at the gates twelve angels, and on the gates are inscribed the names of the twelve tribes of the Israelites; on the east three gates, on the north three gates, on the south three gates, and on the west three gates. And the wall of the city has twelve foundations, and on them are the twelve names of the twelve apostles of the Lamb (Revelation 21:10-14).

Reflection

Most rooms are constructed of four walls and a roof. A door leads us in and out of the room and a window or two allows us to gaze at the world beyond the walls. The walls serve two primary purposes: to keep us or others in or to keep us or others out. Only those we invite through the door can get to our side of the walls.

Besides the walls of homes, we sometimes build walls in our backyards that visually mark where our property line ends and our neighbor's begins. We may build a high redwood fence for privacy or a chain-link fence to keep our dog in the yard or our neighbor's dog out of the yard.

While walls are necessary for our survival and privacy and protection, they can also divide us. After a disagreement, a husband or a wife may go into a room and slam the door, separating themselves from each other. The redwood or chain-link fence in a backyard might represent an unwillingness to meet or get involved with a neighbor.

From God's perspective, walls are not meant for division. The author of the Book of Revelation mentions twelve open gates in God's walls, not built of natural stones, but of human lives. It is in the midst of humankind that God lives. We are precious stones in the city of God. Each of us is unique and, at the same time, an important part of the whole. Just as we display our names outside our homes, so God writes down our names to indicate our unique place in the building of the new Jerusalem.

Meditation

- Make a list of the visible and the invisible walls that separate you from others.
- Identify which walls are good and need to stay in place and which are bad and need to be torn down.
- Identify where you find the living God at work within the walls of your life.

Prayer

God of all creation, no walls can contain you, for you own all of the earth. Yet, in your great mercy you will to live within the walls of my home and, more intimately, within the confines of my heart. Bring peace to my inner being. Root out all that separates me from others. Use me to build the new Jerusalem, where you live and reign with Jesus Christ, your Son, and the Holy Spirit, one God, for ever and ever. Amen.

Water

*A Samaritan woman came to draw water, and Jesus said
to her, "Give me a drink." The Samaritan woman said to
him, "How is it that you, a Jew, ask a drink of me, a
woman of Samaria?" Jesus answered her, "If you knew
the gift of God, and who it is that is saying to you, 'Give
me a drink,' you would have asked him, and he would
have given you living water." The woman said to him,
"Sir, you have no bucket, and the well is deep. Where do
you get that living water? Are you greater than our
ancestor Jacob, who gave us the well, and with his sons
and his flocks drank from it?" Jesus said to her, "Everyone who drinks of this water will be thirsty again, but
those who drink of the water that I will give them will
never be thirsty. The water that I will give will become in
them a spring of water gushing up to eternal life." The
woman said to him, "Sir, give me this water, so that I
may never be thirsty or have to keep coming here to
draw water" (John 4:7, 9-15).*

Reflection

Water is one of our most wasted natural resources. We
use it by the gallon without thinking about it. Rivers,
streams and creeks flow with sparkling water. Gravity tugs
at the ocean and the wind makes the waters wave. From
below the earth, springs bubble up, and man-made wells
place the water at our disposal.

Water flows freely into our kitchens, bathrooms and
laundry rooms, allowing us to bathe, drink, shower, and wash
our clothing. We attach outside faucets and spigots to hoses
and sprinklers that water our lawns and gardens.

We spent our first nine months of existence surrounded by water. The amniotic fluid protected us, nourished us, and permitted us to grow until the water broke forth and we emerged into the world.

On a hot day, we splash and swim in pools and rivers, glide over the waters of a lake in a speedy motorboat, or sit by a river fishing quietly for hours. In winter, when the air is crisp, we put on our skates or skis and enjoy water in its frozen form.

All water reminds us of our baptism. When we wash our hands or the dishes, we remember how we were washed clean of sin and given new life. When we stand at the kitchen sink scrubbing fresh vegetables, when we quench our thirst with a glass of cool water, when we water our plants, we recall how we blossom and grow as we live our baptismal promises. God offers us a stream of grace through Jesus, our "living water." When we drink of it, our thirst is slaked and we become like deep wells overflowing with eternal life.

Meditation

- Place a small bowl of water before you. List the ways you use water in your home.
- Use your list to create a litany of thanksgiving for the gift of water (for example, For the water I drink, thank you, Lord; For the water in which I bathe, thank you Lord; etc.).

Prayer

God of life, you water the mountains and send forth rivers and springs to give drink to every creature. You send showers down on the plains, drenching the furrows, enriching the earth, and making the grain sprout and grow. I hear your voice in the thunder as it rolls over the waters. Let me drink of the living water of your grace through Jesus, your Son, who lives and reigns with you and the Holy Spirit, one God, for ever and ever. Amen.

Windows

Although Daniel knew that the document [prohibiting anyone from addressing any petition to god or man for thirty days, except to King Darius] had been signed, he continued to go to his house, which had windows in its upper room open toward Jerusalem, and to get down on his knees three times a day to pray to his God and praise him, just as he had done previously. The conspirators came and found Daniel praying and seeking mercy before his God (Daniel 6:10-11).

Reflection

Most homes have windows that permit light and air to enter. Windows can be made of clear glass or designed with stained glass to enhance the ambiance of a room.

We stand before a window, gazing out at people walking by, a sunrise or sunset, a leafy tree in the yard, a passing car, a blanket of snow, icicles clinging to the roof, leaves rustling in the wind, or a squirrel scampering around searching for food. In the evening, lights shining through windows give homes a soft, inviting glow.

But our sight can also be distorted by windows. I remember the windows in my great-grandmother's log cabin. The handblown glass panes had bubbles or streaks that threw my vision of the outside world out of focus, altering not only what I saw, but how I perceived reality.

Such windows remind us of biases, presuppositions, rumors, lifetime experiences, and limitations that distort not only what we see, but how we see.

Even our idea of God is limited by the various windows we look through. Some see God as an angry old man, out to get us if we stray. Others see God as a benevolent father who watches over us. Some see God as a mother who nourishes and nurtures us.

The best window through which to see God is an open one. Only in that way can God enter our world and we enter God's world.

Meditation

- Kneel before a window in your home. List everything and everyone you see.
- For each item or person on your list, identify how God is revealed to you.
- When you are finished, go outside and see what you could not see through your window. Identify how God is also revealed in these things and people.

Prayer

O Lord, before I was born you gave me the gift of sight so that I might recognize your presence in all of your creation. Do not let the windows of my vision become hindrances. Rather, let me see clearly the beauty that stretches out before my gaze, that my lips might proclaim your praise. Lead me into prayer every hour of the day through Jesus Christ, your Son, who lives and reigns with you and the Holy Spirit, one God, for ever and ever. Amen.

Xerox

All the people gathered together into the square before the Water Gate. They told the scribe Ezra to bring the book of the law of Moses, which the L<small>ORD</small> had given to Israel. Accordingly, the priest Ezra brought the law before the assembly, both men and women and all who could hear with understanding....He read from it facing the square before the Water Gate from early morning until midday, in the presence of the men and the women and those who could understand; and the ears of all the people were attentive to the book of the law (Nehemiah 8:1-3).

Reflection

Before Xerox machines, there were typewriters and carbon paper, "ditto" machines and stencils. And before any of these devices, there were blackboards and chalk, papyrus leaves and scrolls, parchments and clay tablets. In biblical times, a scribe took stylus, quill or pen and hand copied a book or a manuscript. Throughout history, people have copied the written word.

While there is a variety of copiers and printers on the market today, most of us refer to copying as "xeroxing," a process which photographs an original document and develops it onto a clean sheet of paper. The process has become so widespread that many homes contain personal copiers.

Much of the material we receive in the mail is xeroxed. Bills, letters, memos, advertisements, articles from magazines, music, and pages from books are the result of our ability to xerox. By receiving and making copies of the printed word, we preserve the text for later reading or study, feeding our minds in the present while securing the possibility of reviewing the same documents in the future.

Xeroxing can make us aware of the presence of God by reminding us of the availability of God's word. In the past, people had to listen as the word of God was read from a community copy of the Bible. We imitate this ancient practice at Mass, when the lector, deacon and priest proclaim the word to us while we sit or stand attentively.

However, because of today's easy availability of the word of God, we can read it ahead of time and read it often. The word feeds our eyes, minds and hearts. As we xerox it from the Bible and onto our lives, we become a copy of Jesus, who represents all that we are called to be.

Meditation

- Copy your favorite passage from the Bible and tack it where you will see it every day (for example, on the refrigerator door, bathroom mirror, etc.).
- List the ways this passage is being "imprinted" onto your life. In other words, how are you living the word of God?

Prayer

Lord God, you have spoken your word through the law and the prophets. In the fullness of time your eternal Word, Jesus Christ, became man and taught me how to make my life a copy of your will. Give me understanding when I read your word. Give me discernment to know your will. Give me the courage to live what I believe. Imprint upon me the image of Jesus, your Son, who lives and reigns with you and the Holy Spirit, one God, for ever and ever. Amen.

Yarn

O LORD, you have searched me and known me.
You know when I sit down and when I rise up;
    you discern my thoughts from far away.
You search out my path and my lying down,
    and are acquainted with all my ways.
Even before a word is on my tongue,
    O LORD, you know it completely.
You hem me in, behind and before,
    and lay your hand upon me.
Such knowledge is too wonderful for me;
    it is so high that I cannot attain it.
Where can I go from your spirit?
    Or where can I flee from your presence?
If I ascend to heaven, you are there;
    if I make my bed in Sheol, you are there.
If I take the wings of the morning
    and settle at the farthest limits of the sea,
even there your hand shall lead me,
    and your right hand shall hold me fast....
For it was you who formed my inward parts;
    you knit me together in my mother's womb.
I praise you, for I am fearfully and wonderfully made.
    Wonderful are your works;
that I know very well.
    My frame was not hidden from you,
  when I was being made in secret,
    intricately woven in the depths of the earth.

                                                                        Psalm 139:1-10, 13-15

Reflection

In the closet where I keep my packaging supplies is a bag filled with pieces of yarn. Once used to decorate gifts given to me, these will now be used on gifts I will give to others.

We usually buy yarn in a skein, which has to be unraveled and formed into a ball for easier handling. Yarn is used for knitting and crocheting afghans, doilies, sweaters, socks, sock caps, booties and slippers. It is also used in school art classes to put the finishing touch on a project, and some women tie up their hair with a length of yarn.

Each of our lives are like a length of yarn that has been knitted together with all who enter our home. Family members and friends are all permanently woven into the fabric-of-our-life tapestry.

Also knitted into our lives is God, whose presence in our lives began the moment we were conceived and will continue even beyond the grave. There is no place where God is not present and woven intricately into our lives.

Meditation

- Look around and list items in your home that are made with yarn. For each, indicate someone with whom you associate the item.
- How is each person woven into the fabric of your life (and home)? In what way(s) has each person influenced you? Into whose lives are you woven?

Prayer

O Lord, you formed me in my mother's womb and knit me together in the secret recesses of your heart. You have been my guide since the day I was born; on you I depend for my strength. Give me a greater respect for all who have been knitted into my life and make me ever aware of your presence. I praise and thank you through Jesus Christ, your Son, who lives and reigns with you and the Holy Spirit, one God, for ever and ever. Amen.

Zipper

Israel loved Joseph more than any other of his children, because he was the son of his old age; and he had made him a long robe with sleeves. But when his brothers saw that their father loved him more than all his brothers, they hated him, and could not speak peaceably to him.

...They saw him from a distance, and before he came near to them, they conspired to kill him....So when Joseph came to his brothers, they stripped him of his robe, the long robe with sleeves that he wore; and they took him and threw him into a pit. The pit was empty; there was no water in it.

Then they sat down to eat; and looking up they saw a caravan of Ishmaelites coming from Gilead....They drew Joseph up, lifting him out of the pit, and sold him to the Ishmaelites for twenty pieces of silver.

Then they took Joseph's robe, slaughtered a goat, and dipped the robe in the blood. They had the long robe with sleeves taken to their father, and they said, "This we have found; see now whether it is your son's robe or not." He recognized it, and said, "It is my son's robe! A wild animal has devoured him; Joseph is without doubt torn to pieces!" (Genesis 37:3-4, 18, 23-25, 28, 31-33).

Reflection

Next to buttons, the most common means of opening and closing clothing and other items are zippers. We zip up our coats, sweaters, dresses, shirts and trousers. We use zippers to secure storage bags, luggage, and personal tote bags. Even in the kitchen, a zipper is used on sandwich and freezer bags.

Our lives have something resembling zippers that can be opened to permit people to enter or closed to keep people out. Through our "life-zippers" we allow knowledge, experience and faith to enter and change us, or we exclude them. Even as children, we learned to use these zippers. If we had a secret to keep, we'd "zip up our lips" to indicate that we would not tell a soul.

The zipper to God's life and love is always open. And even if we frustrate God's plan, as did Joseph's brothers, God can unzip our lives and bring forth good, as Joseph ultimately opened his heart, forgave his brothers, and saved them from famine. For only through an open heart can the Spirit enter our lives, fill them with grace, and motivate us to follow God's will.

Meditation

- List three recent experiences of zipping closed your life. List three recent experiences of zipping open your life.
- Who was involved and what did you learn from the experience? How was God present?

Prayer

Lord, my strength, my rock, my fortress, my deliverer, my refuge, my shield, my salvation, my stronghold. I praise you for keeping me safe. You remembered your people, Israel, and sent Joseph, sold as a slave, into Egypt, where he learned to forgive and to love. Zipper me within the cloak of your grace. I ask this through Jesus Christ, your Son, who lives and reigns with you and the Holy Spirit, one God, for ever and ever. Amen.

Also Available From ACTA Publications

The Greatest Gift of All: Reflections and Prayers for the Christmas Season
Mark G. Boyer

Here is another wonderful collection of forty-two reflections by Fr. Boyer, this time focusing on objects and themes that surround the Christmas season. (112 pages, $8.95)

A Month-by-Month Guide to Entertaining Angels
Mark G. Boyer

Filled with information about thirty-six amazing encounters with angels that have been recorded in the Bible, this book explains how heavenly messengers reveal God's loving presence in people's lives today. (192 pages, $11.95)

Grace Is Everywhere: Reflections of an Aspiring Monk
James Stephen Behrens, O.C.S.O.

This best-selling first book of vignettes by a Trappist monk of the Monastery of the Holy Spirit in Conyers, Georgia, explores the connection between monastic spirituality and everyday life. (160 pages, $9.95)

Daily Meditations Series

These daily meditation books combine down-to-earth reflections with illuminating verses from the Scriptures. Separate books for Busy Moms, Dads, Grandmas, Grandpas and Couples. (368 pages each, $8.95 each)

**Available from religious book sellers
or call 800-397-2282 in the U.S. or Canada.**